AF447999

Rotimi Oluwaseyitan

Dealing with the Spirit of Herod

Victory Over the Enemy of Progress

For information contact:
ROTIMI OLUWASEYITAN MINISTRIES INC.
1843 Arboretum Circle Vestavia Hills, Alabama 35216.
Email: pastorrotimi@outlook.com
Website: www.pastorrotimi.org

ROTIMI OLUWASEYITAN MINISTRIES
Ghana: 16th street Collins Dauda Road, Community 18
Tema, Accra Ghana

ROTIMI OLUWASEYITAN MINISTRIES
Asia: Vista Pinggiran Putra 43300 Seri Kembangan
Malaysia

DEDICATION

This e-book is dedicated to family, friends, and partners of Rotimi Oluwaseyitan Ministries Inc.

Chapter One
Who is Herod

Herod is a popular name in bible days, among the Jews and the early Christians. The name means heroic, and it is popularly associated with a family, who is known for power, politics, immorality, and continuous clashes. There are about seven individuals in the family, who by virtue of their position and wicked disposition in the society, made the name Herod popular.

Herod the great:
This was Herod, who got to know about the birth of baby Jesus, through the wise men from the East. He was so much intimidated and infuriated about the news of Jesus' birth, that he slew all the children from two years and under, in an attempt to destroy Jesus Christ. (Matthew 2:1).

Herod Archelaus:

This was the Herod that was on the throne, when Joseph returned to Jerusalem from Egypt, with Mary and Jesus Christ, according to God's instructions. He was the son of Herod the Great, who sought for baby Jesus to destroy Him. (Matthew 2:22).

Herod Tetrarch:

Herod Tetrarch, is also known as Herod Antipas. This was the Herod whom John the Baptist rebuked for taking his brother's wife, and who gave John's head as a present to Herodias' daughter, for impressing him with a dance, during his birthday party. The Pharisees used his name to threaten Jesus, in the course of His ministry. He was also involved in Jesus' trial. (Matthew 14:1-11, Mark 6:14-28, 8:15; Luke 3:1, 19-20, 9:7-9, 13:31-33, 23:5-16, Acts 4:27, 13:1).

Herod Philip:

This Herod was the son of Herod the Great. He was the original husband of Herodias, whom his brother Herod the Antipas took from him. (Matthew 14:3, Mark 6:17-18; Luke 3:1).

Herod the Agrippa 1:

This was the grandson of Herod the Great. This was the Herod, who arrested and executed James. He also arrested Peter, and kept him in the prison, with the intention of executing him after the Passover; but God overtook him in his plan, in response to the prayer of the church. (Acts 12:1-23).

Herod the Agrippa 2:
This was the Herod, before whom Paul's case was brought. It was the Herod who said that Paul almost succeeded in persuading him, to become a Christian (Acts 25:13-26:32).

Going through the scriptures, and events in the bible, about everyone who took on, the title Herod; there seems to be a spirit behind the title, that automatically controls each of the people, as they came into the office.

The spirit may be called by any name, but it can always be identified, or discerned by its manifestation. The spirit can manifest through anyone, who opens himself or herself to it.

Chapter Two

The Manifestation of the Spirit of Herod

#1 The spirit of Herod is provoked when he hears about your testimony

"When Herod the king had heard these things, he was troubled, and all Jerusalem with him." (Matthew 2:3 KJV)

What could provoke a king to anger, with the news about a baby? Even if the baby is going to be a king, it will take the next thirty years for it, to be a reality.

Have you noticed, that there are certain individuals, who are provoked with your testimonies for no reason? They could not just endure seeing God answering your prayer, or promoting you.

Their mood automatically changes, once they hear what God is doing in your life. You must look beyond the man, or woman, who is reacting to your testimonies, there is a spirit in operation in their lives, called the spirit of Herod.

It is the spirit of Herod, that makes a man, or woman, become unnecessarily unhappy and annoyed, at another person's testimony of increase, promotion, advancement, for no reason.

The fact is, this spirit can operate through anyone, who has not dealt with their flesh. As believers, we must be watchful, that we don't open ourselves up to the spirit of Herod.

The Bible says, we must rejoice with those who are rejoicing. Once you start feeling funny towards your brother, or sister's testimony, something is wrong somewhere. It is the manifestation of the spirit of Herod; resist it immediately, in the name of Jesus Christ.

#2 The spirit of Herod operates through informants to gather information about you

"Then Herod, when he had privily called the wise men, enquired of them diligently what time the star appeared. And he sent them to Bethlehem, and said, Go

and search diligently for the young child; and when ye have found him, bring me word again, that I may come and worship him also." (Matthew 2:7-8 KJV).

The devil is not omniscient, so the spirit of Herod thrives through the network of informants. All gossips and backbiting can be traced to the manifestation of the spirit of Herod.   People that suddenly become uncontrollably inquisitive, and nosy into other people's affairs, are under the influence of the spirit of Herod.

When people are not comfortable with, what the Lord is doing in your life, they become unreasonably interested in what is happening in your life. They will employ every means to get information about you.

You have to be sensitive, and discerning in your interaction with people. Not everyone should get access to the privacy of God's plan and purpose for your life.

When people start asking too much detail about the event of your life, you must learn to wisely change the topic, and address the spirit that is attempting to dig into the secret and strength of your story.

#3 The spirit of Herod always seeks to kill anything newly birthed or started

"And when they were departed, behold, the angel of the Lord appeareth to Joseph in a dream, saying, Arise, and take the young child and his mother, and flee into Egypt, and be thou there until I bring thee word: for Herod will seek the young child to destroy him." (Mat 2:13 KJV)

When you see people walking under the influence of the spirit of Herod, they are always comfortable with the old you, but the new you is always a threat to them.

They could be very friendly with you, as long as nothing new is happening in your life. The moment you start something new, you will begin to see the other side of them.

The spirit can manifest through leaders, co-workers or labourers. It could operate in organizations, and even in the church. Whenever any new thing is birthed, the spirit of Herod will always rise to kill it. New ideas do not prosper, where the spirit of Herod is operating.

Where the spirit of Herod is operational, young ministry, young business, young marriage, young dream, or young vision, suffer and struggle to thrive, because people under the influence of the spirit of

Herod, go all out, to see that anything young or new does not survive.

So, sometimes when you notice someone manifesting the spirit of Herod, it is wise to take your young business, and new idea far away from them.

#4 The spirit of Herod will seek to destroy everything around you when he fails to get you

"Then Herod, when he saw that he was mocked of the wise men, was exceeding wroth, and sent forth, and slew all the children that were in Bethlehem, and in all the coasts thereof, from two years old and under, according to the time which he had diligently enquired of the wise men." (Matthew 2:16 KJV)

When Herod failed to get baby Jesus, he went all out, against every child from two years of age and under. People under the influence of the spirit of Herod, can destroy everything around you, in their attempt to get at you.

When they fail in their attempt to destroy you, they will destroy anything they can touch around you. When they fail to destroy your ministry, they will try your marriage.

When they fail to destroy your business, they will attempt your reputation.

I remember some years back precisely 2008. I was travelling to a country in Asia, for a preaching engagement, but unknown to me certain individuals have gone to the airport to give the police false information about me.

The police at the airport received information about me, that I will be travelling with drugs. They were informed that I swallowed it, and I also have it packed in my luggage. They told them the date I will be travelling, the time of my flight, the airline, and my destination.

I got to the airport, checked in and I was on my way to board, when I was apprehended by the police. I was in the police custody for three days for a thorough investigation.

I was released after three days, and given a certificate of clearance, that I did not carry any drugs. But I could no longer travel that month, and scheduled it for the following month, in agreement with the church, that I supposed to preach for.

I was in my office one day browsing and searching for something on google when I noticed that my name appeared on a gay site, and when I clicked on it, they have filled my information with my picture on a gay site, that I am looking for a man of the same age, who may be ready for a date. I was dumbfounded.

When I contacted the owner of the website, they claimed that there are many people that answer that name, but by now, they have removed, and replaced my picture with another person's picture.

I guess, the plan of the person who did all these, was to discredit me, before the church I will be preaching for in Asia, in case they search for me online.

When the people under the influence of the spirit of Herod fail to get you, they will attempt to destroy everything around you.

#5 The spirit of Herod will cause men to unlawfully take what belongs to you.

"For Herod had laid hold on John, and bound him, and put him in prison for Herodias' sake, his brother Philip's wife. For John said unto him, It is not lawful for thee to have her." (Mat 14:3-4 KJV)

Herod has his wife, but he preferred his brother's wife. There are many women in the town, that he could have picked from, but it was his brother's wife, he preferred. He used all his power and influence, to take the woman from him.

 One of the major characteristics of the spirit of Herod, is covetousness. When you see people under the spirit of Herod, they are highly covetous people. They have their car, but they want your own. They have their wife, but they prefer yours.

They may not like that shoe, until they see it with you. They may not like that apartment, until you are the one living in there. They are ready to use all the power, and the resources at their disposal, to negotiate a new contract with your landlord to evict you.

People who take what does not belong to them, either by trick, or by threat, are operating under the spirit of Herod. People who rob and kidnap, are controlled by the spirit of Herod.

Don't wait for them to take from you before you, rise in prayer against the spirit, that rules in their lives.

#6 The spirit of Herod is a destiny mocker, He rejoices at your fall and your pain

"And Herod with his men of war set him at nought, and mocked him, and arrayed him in a gorgeous robe, and sent him again to Pilate. And the same day Pilate and Herod were made friends together: for before they were at enmity between themselves." (Luke 23:11-12 KJV)

When Herod saw that they finally got Jesus, it pleased him, and gladdened his heart. He mocked Jesus. Herod was provoked when he heard about the testimony of Jesus' birth, but mocked when he saw that Jesus was arrested. Herod negotiated and reconciled with his enemy, in his attempt to achieve his mission against Jesus.

The people walking under the influence of the spirit of Herod, find pleasure in the downfall of others. If you find yourself happy, when your brother suffers or falls, you are operating under the spirit of Herod.

If your response to the news about your brother's, or sister's failure, or disappointment, was God pays him or her well; you have a problem with the spirit of Herod. You must deal with it.

God does not look with kindness, with those who rejoice at other people's predicament. Love does not rejoice at evil and unrighteousness. Love rejoices when right and truth prevail.

God dealt with the descendants of Esau, for rejoicing at the calamity of the children of Isreal. God rebuked them, for holding down their brothers for their enemies, in the day that the enemy besieged their cities.

#7 The spirit of Herod seeks to take the glory that belongs to God in your life

"And the people gave a shout, saying, It is the voice of a god, and not of a man. (Act 12:23 KJV) And immediately the angel of the Lord smote him, because he gave not God the glory: and he was eaten of worms, and gave up the ghost." (Act 12:22-23 KJV)

Herod has been of great help to the people of Tyre and Sidon, but he did not consider that his ability to help, and assist came from the Lord. Rather than returning the glory to the Lord, when the people ascribed the glory to him, he accepted it as his own, and was smitten by the angel of the Lord, and eaten by worms.

God must be glorified in anything good, that can be ascribed to our ability or generosity. When you find yourself seeking to be praised and honoured, for anything good in anyone's life, you are opening yourself up, to the spirit of Herod; bind that spirit immediately. When men and women begin to praise you, for one thing, or the other, be quick to point them back to the Lord, from whom all good things come.

The spirit of Herod will always want people to take the glory that belongs to God. He pushes people into a position where they think they can no longer wait for God again, and they have to see that person, or that uncle for help, as such their testimony is not complete without saying, if not for Uncle Dee and Brother Zee.

People who are under the influence of the spirit of Herod, are never satisfied, until their praise and their names are mentioned in association with your testimony.

Chapter Three

How to Deal with the Spirit of Herod

Prayer Power
"Peter, therefore, was kept in prison: but prayer was made without ceasing of the church unto God for him." (Act 12:5 KJV)

Herod and the power of the days, were not pleased with the testimony of the growth of the early church. Herod arrested James, and executed him, because the church underrated the wickedness of the spirit of Herod.

When he arrested Peter, the church said not again, it cannot be. The church rose up in a corporate, and consistent prayer against the spirit of Herod and Herod's expectation was disappointed by the Lord.

Prayer still works, it does not matter the degree of wickedness mobilized against you, when you rise up in the spirit of prayer, any power of the enemy can be subdued.

Angelic Assistance

"And upon a set day Herod, arrayed in royal apparel, sat upon his throne, and made an oration unto them. And the people gave a shout, saying, It is the voice of a god, and not of a man. And immediately the angel of the Lord smote him, because he gave not God the glory: and he was eaten of worms, and gave up the ghost. But the word of God grew and multiplied." (Act 12:21-24 KJV)

Part of the effect of prayer power, was the final destruction of Herod. The angel of the Lord smote Herod and worms ate him up.

Angels are always ready to rise, for the assistance of the heirs of salvation. They run an errand for the children of God. Employ the service of the angel of God against, any activities of the spirit of Herod, in and around your life.

Don't keep quiet in the face of any harassment of the enemy. The angels of God are waiting to run an errand for you against the enemy; deploy your angel to disappoint the operation of the enemy against your life.

Prophetic declaration

"The same day there came certain of the Pharisees, saying unto him, Get thee out, and depart hence: for Herod will kill thee. And he said unto them, Go ye, and tell that fox, Behold, I cast out devils, and I do cures today and tomorrow, and the third day I shall be perfected. Nevertheless, I must walk to day, and tomorrow and the day following: for it cannot be that a prophet perish out of Jerusalem." (Luk 13:31-33 KJV)

Look at how our Lord Jesus Christ handled the spirit of Herod. When they threatened Jesus to run out of the city, because Herod is seeking to kill Him. He replied to them, with some prophetic declaration, about His ministry and assignment.

Locate scriptures that promise you victory, and dominion, over whatever the enemy is trying to destroy in your life, and declare boldly the scriptures against the enemy.

Chapter Four

Prayers Against the Spirit of Herod

PRAYER POINTS

Father, let every power assigned against my progress will be arrested, and be destroyed, in the name of Jesus Christ.

Father, let every informant commissioned to collect data about what You are doing in my life, career, business, and ministry be frustrated, in the name of Jesus Christ.

Father, I pray that the helpers of my destiny, shall not miss their ways, nor fall into the trap of the spirit of Herod, in the name of Jesus Christ.

Father, let every attempt to terminate my life, by the spirit of Herod backfire on the enemy, in the name of Jesus Christ.

Father, I pray that my vessels of assistance, shall not cooperate, nor yield to the manipulation of the spirit of Herod, in the name of Jesus Christ.

I declare and decree, that I shall not be a puppet, or victim of the spirit of Herod, in Jesus' name.

Father, I employ the ministry of the angels, against every power, attempting to share the glory of God in my life, in the name of Jesus Christ.

I declare and decree, that whatever the enemy has seen, or heard concerning my life, that may trouble them shall come to reality against their desires, in the name of Jesus Christ.

I declare and decree, that helpers shall locate my star, and everything that belongs to me, shall come to me in the name of Jesus Christ.

About the Author

Rotimi is a Pastor, church planter, an author and a Chris- tian Devotional Writer. He is the President and Founder of Rotimi Oluwaseyitan Ministries. He has been in full-time ministries since 1994 and served in various capacities in Nigeria and Benin Republic before he was sent by the Lord to Asia in 2012, for the next phase of his assignment. He is happily married to Adeyinka Oluwaseyitan